Colours of
Bhutan

First and second editions published in Bhutan in 2006 and 2008 by

Jomo Publications
Kawajangsa
Thimphu - Bhutan
E-mail: jomo@druknet.bt

Editor: Jomo Publications, Thimphu
Design: Jean-Christophe Monnier

ISBN: 99936-683-0-3

Colours of
Bhutan

Text and photographs
Robert Dompnier

 **JOMO** PUBLICATIONS

Contents

Foreword

Colours of Bhutan... a host of expressions could be used to evoke the natural and cultural beauty of Bhutan... Yet the first-time visitor is struck primarily by the colour of this small Himalayan kingdom. With its snow-capped mountains, lakes and glaciers, forests, jungles and exceptional flora, Bhutan offers a natural environment of rare diversity. In this unique setting, the Bhutanese have created a world of colours, shades and hues that infuse their architecture, their daily life and their religious festivals. Their costumes and fabrics are an integral part of this colourful world, which leaves no room for the monotonous and drab. Crossing Bhutan from west to east or north to south is a real feast for the eyes.

And it is a paradise for photographers. As elsewhere in the Himalayas, the gentle light of spring or autumn, the heavy skies of summer and the first snows of winter provide an endless range of subjects, constantly changing in shape and colour. Here, photography truly becomes a form of witness, a way of revealing the beauty of the environment but also a means of discovering the cultural identity of the country. Bhutan's culture and traditions are immensely rich and offer a limitless source of inspiration. And last but not least, the photographer can capture the character traits of the people - their omnipresent smiles and serene faces clearly expressing their deep faith in the words and teachings of Buddha.

Perusing a book of photographs makes us realise that images often speak a thousand words and that a good picture can replace many a long speech... Instead of endless pages of text trying to describe or convince, photography summarises, synthesises and takes us to the heart of the matter. It also invites us to travel and fires our imagination. May this book enrich its readers as they discover a secret, unique and endearing country, a kingdom rich of many colours...

Robert Dompnier,
Chambery (France), October 2005

A brief history of Bhutan

Nestling in the heart of the Himalayas and protected by a complex geography of high mountains and deep valleys, Bhutan is certainly one of the most mysterious countries in the world. Impenetrable jungle to the south and daunting ranges of snow-capped mountains to the north have long barred all access to this tiny kingdom for many centuries. In spite of many battles with the Tibeto-Mongol armies or the troops of the British Empire stationed in India, the country has never been colonised since the 8th century. Bhutan has therefore kept alive its extremely rich heritage of traditions, which in broad outline resemble those of Tibetan civilisation. About the same size as Switzerland, this kingdom of just under a million people has doggedly kept itself apart from the restlessness of the modern world, proud of its own values and traditions.

The Bhutanese call their country "Druk Yul", the Land of the Dragon, or more exactly the land of the drukpas who forged its unity in the 17th century. The drukpas, a branch of the kagyupas, took their name from the monastery of Druk, founded in 1189 by Tsangpa Gyare at a spot near Lhasa where legend says a dragon appeared.

The development of Buddhism

One has to wait until the 7th century to find the earliest texts referring to Bhutan. They relate the construction of the temples at Kyichu in the Paro valley and Jampa Lhakhang in that of Bumthang by the Tibetan king Songtsen Gampo, who reigned from 627 to 650. Through these acts, the monarch helped to spread Buddhism in the "southern valleys" where at that time animist and shamanic religions prevailed.

But it was with the arrival of the great Indian master Padmasambhava in the 8th century that Buddhism really began to spread throughout this Himalayan land. Known as Guru Rimpoche by the Bhutanese and Tibetans, Padmasambhava is said to have arrived in Bhutan in 747, invited to the country to cure a king who was on his deathbed. He meditated, taught Buddhism and had several temples built. The places he visited are still venerated today. Moreover, Padmasambhava hid sacred texts in various parts of the country; their profound meaning was incomprehensible to the people of the period. "Treasure-finders" known as tertöns in the local language would be led to discover them much later so as to complete the master's teaching and finish his work. With the coming of Padmasambhava, Buddhism began gradually to replace the local cults, sometimes incorporating certain beliefs from them. In the 9th century, many Tibetan lords who had fled to Bhutan joined the native people converted earlier. Buddhists in Tibet were persecuted during the reign of King Langdarma and these lords settled in the east of the country, where they formed small principalities.

The unification of the country

In 1616, due to a quarrel over the succession to the throne of Ralung, the seat of the drukpa-kagyu order in Tibet, Ngawang Namgyel had to flee to Bhutan. His arrival marked a major turning point in the country's history and organisation. Ngawang Namgyel, who is still referred to as Shabdrung "He at whose feet one submits", quickly imposed his political and religious authority throughout western Bhutan. In just a few years, he succeeded in bringing together all the independent principalities and initiating a process of unification. When he died in 1651 order had been restored almost everywhere.

The great fortresses of Simtokha, Punakha, Wangdiphodrang and Tongsa were built during his reign. While ensuring the country's safety, they also served as relays for the central authority and its administration.

Resisting many invasions by the Tibetans and Mongols during the course of his reign, Ngawang Namgyel quickly became both feared and admired inside Bhutan and beyond its borders. His great sense of organisation enabled him to introduce order into the monasteries and to set up a religious hierarchy dominated by the Je Khenpo. He appointed a regent, the Desi, to head the civil administration, giving him temporal power throughout the country. This double system of government, known as chhoesi, remained in force in Bhutan until the creation of the hereditary monarchy in 1907. Because of his legacy in terms of administrative, legislative and religious reforms, Ngawang Namgyel is considered to be the principal architect of modern Bhutan.

The establishment of the monarchy

After a century of domestic strife and warfare against the British Raj, Ugyen Wangchuck became the undisputed master of the country. He then started a long process to strengthen the central power in order to recover the unity that Ngawang Namgyel had achieved 250 years before. He gradually rallied all the lords throughout the country to his cause and on 17 December 1907 was proclaimed King of Bhutan by an assembly including representatives of the clergy, Council of State and local governors. He took the title of Druk Gyalpo, thus ending the system of chhoesi. The position of Desi disappeared and only that of Je Khenpo remained as the spiritual leader of Bhutan.

But a new era really began with King Jigme Dorje Wangchuck, the third monarch to rule over the country. Born in 1928, he was crowned king in 1952. A reformer and man of progress, one of his first acts was to set up a national assembly in 1953. Known as the tshogdu, this comprised representatives of the people, civil administration and clergy. Other bodies were created one after another, in particular the Royal Council and a Council of Ministers. Jigme Dorje Wangchuck separated the judiciary from the executive, creating a High Court of Justice, and abolished serfdom.

His Majesty Jigme Singye Wangchuck was born in 1955 and, when he succeeded his father, became the youngest monarch in the world. He was crowned in 1974 and has since continued a policy of development and modernisation while taking care to preserve the natural and cultural heritage of his country. On many occasions, he has demonstrated his determination to give greater responsibility to the Bhutanese people, by creating elected decision-making bodies in the villages and districts. A further proof of this desire to involve the people more was the 1998 Royal Decree giving power to the National Assembly to ratify or reject the nomination of Ministers, who were hitherto appointed solely at the King's discretion. While the third King was the father of modern Bhutan, Jigme Singye Wangchuck seems destined to be the father of democracy. He wisely prepared Bhutan to enter the 21st century, maintaining a harmonious balance between a respect for tradition and a commitment to economic development. Bhutan is currently drafting a parliamentary constitution and is paving the way to a multi-party system.

Dominating the Indian plain, Bhutan rises stage by stage, step by step, hill by hill, from the luxuriant jungles in the south to the dizzy summits of the Himalayan range. Over a north-south distance of about 170 km, these differences in altitude produce a great diversity of climates and an extreme variety of environments, sometimes placing sub-tropical vegetation next to glaciers. Most Bhutanese villages are built in the medium-altitude valleys and are surrounded by cultivated fields. The main crop is rice, as here in the Tashigang region (right). Sometimes, they are located in the high glaciated valleys, like Thangza, situated in the heart of the Lunana region (following double page).

Environment

The snow-capped peaks of the high Himalayas dominate the north of the kingdom. A dozen summits rise to over 7000 metres. Many of them have never been climbed and remain the inviolate homes of the gods. A few villages are to be found in this harsh mountain region, home to the semi-nomadic Layap, Lunap or Brokpa shepherds of Merak and Sakteng.

Above: Gangkar Puensum (7541 m), the highest summit in Bhutan, seen from a small pass above Warthang.

Right: a Layap with his caravan of yaks arrives in the village of Woche.

Opposite: the Lunana region boasts many lakes ranging in colour from turquoise to emerald.

Bhutan has been blessed by the gods with ample water resources. Many glaciers and natural lakes in the north of the country give rise to swift torrents and quieter rivers that water the entire country.

Top: houses amid the fields on the road to Bumthang.

Right: forest on the path to Laya.

Opposite: after passing at the foot of Wangdiphodrang *dzong*, the river Puna Tsang chu runs southwards and crosses the Indian frontier before flowing into a tributary of the Brahmaputra.

Following double page: cultivated fields opposite the village of Rhadi.

Bhutan is a paradise for fauna and flora, and specialists from all over the world come to study nature. Wildlife is rich and varied. Ten reserves, representing about 20% of the total area of Bhutan, have been created to protect species that are sometimes extremely rare. While the jungles in the south are home to elephants, single-horned rhinoceros, tigers, buffaloes and monkeys, including the famous golden langur, the mountains in the centre are the refuge of deer, white-collared bears, boars and red pandas. Blue sheep graze in the high pastures at the edge of the glaciers, where the snow leopard hides among the rocks.

Thanks to the heavy monsoon rains, Bhutan is densely wooded, with tropical jungle in the south giving way to mountain forests in the north. From March to October, the northern forests are ablaze with an infinite variety of flowers such as rhododendron or the famous blue poppy (Meconopsis horridula).

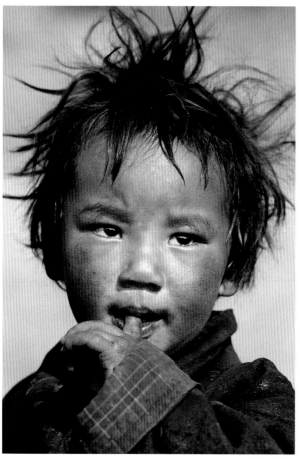

The great fortresses known as *dzong* are among the most striking examples of Bhutanese architecture. Built in the first half of the 17th century by Shabdrung Ngawang Namgyel, they acted as relays for the central authority and helped it in running the country, while at the same time fending off any attacks from beyond its borders.

Symbolising the history and long independence of Bhutan, the *dzong* rise proudly in strategic places, at the entrance to a valley, at the summit of a hill or at the confluence of two rivers.

Opposite: surrounded by flowering jacarandas, Punakha *dzong* is an architectural wonder, with its many richly decorated windows and balconies.

Following double page; Paro *dzong* dominates the village and controls the valley.

Architecture

Tashichhodzong, the "fortress of the auspicious religion", was built in the 18th century and enlarged in the 1960s after the third King of Bhutan, His Majesty Jigme Dorji Wangchuck, decided to make Thimphu his permanent capital. Today, it is the seat of the Royal Government of Bhutan. The *dzong* overlooks a quaint old wooden bridge spanning the waters of the river.

The building that can be seen today consists of a two-storeyed oblong structure, surrounding the central courtyard. Imposing towers stand at the four corners and the central axis through the *dzong* runs almost exactly north-south. A special feature found only in Tashichhodzong are the separate entrances to the monastic and administrative sections. The four towers at the corners consist of a ground and first floor with walls of dressed stone, topped off with a timber superstructure, which projects on all four sides over the lower storeys. These projecting walls of the third storey are supported by a fully traditional assembly of excellently carved timber elements.

Today, next to the Cabinet of His Majesty the King and the offices of the Royal Advisory Council, only the Ministries of the Interior and Finance have remained in Tashichhodzong. The Ministries of Foreign Affairs and Planning have moved into the new SAARC building constructed in the 1990s.

Opposite: an architectural masterpiece, Tongsa *dzong* rises in stages up the side of a hill overlooking the river Mangde chu. It was built in 1644 by Minjur Tenpa on the site of a temple erected a century earlier by Ngagi Wangchuck. Tongsa has been constantly enlarged and today comprises more than 20 temples. From the outside, it looks mostly like a defensive structure. Its great stone walls lean very slightly inwards, rising shear up to the roof. Massive and steep, they are broken only by high windows that are totally inaccessible from outside. Just below the roof, a wide red stripe, known as *khemar,* recalls the religious nature of the building. Inside these outer walls, the main courtyard is surrounded by two- or three- storey buildings. The courtyard itself is normally paved with large stone flags. In the middle of the courtyard stands a massive tower known as *utse*. It is much taller than the other buildings and resembles the keep of medieval castles in Europe. The upper floors of this tower house the various temples, known as *lhakhang*

Above: while the external structure is intentionally austere, the richly decorated arcades, galleries and balconies are typical features of the buildings inside a *dzong*. Behind them are the monks' quarters and administrative offices.

Following double page: painted walls in one of the inner courtyards of Paro *dzong*.

The wall decorations and sculptures inside the *dzongs* are often rich and colourful. The subjects are drawn from traditional Bhutanese religious myths and legends.

Above: Mongol holding a yak on a tether (Paro *dzong*)

Right: astrological calendar and skilfully worked balcony (Punakha *dzong*)

Opposite page: the famous monastery of Taktsang, clinging to the rock face, is also a magnificent example of Bhutanese architecture. This is one of the holiest places in Bhutan.
Taktsang, the tiger's lair, derives its name from its foundation. According to tradition, Guru Rinpoche came here in the 8th century on the back of a flying tigress. He meditated in a cave at Taktsang and converted the Paro valley to Buddhism.

Some of the commonest structures in Bhutan are the *chorten,* which are known as *stupa* in India. There are thousands of these monuments all over the country, ranging in size from the very small to the very large. Witnesses to the profound faith of the Bhutanese, they can be found at cross-roads, near a *dzong* or a monastery and on high mountain passes.
They all have an indefinable presence, radiating serenity and peace like this *chorten* at Kurichu (right).

In its essence, each *chorten* has a precise symbolism, the meaning of which can be interpreted at several levels. It is first of all a monument commemorating the death (Parinirvâna) of the Buddha Sakyamuni. But it also symbolises the universe, which consists of a combination of five elements, earth, water, fire, air and finally ether, the essence of the spirit. This deep essence of things is seized by means of the *dharma,* which leads the adept through the last stages of his spiritual progress towards enlightenment. One of the five *Jina* or *Dhyâni-Buddha,* the primordial Buddha, corresponds to each of these elements. For religious and didactic reasons, the *chorten* has always been an object of faith and devotion for the entire Buddhist world.

Bhutanese society is extremely egalitarian and as such has no rigid class structure. Anyone can rise through the ranks of the civil service or private sector. Bhutanese women enjoy equivalent rights to men, taking an active part in the affairs of the country and sometimes holding high positions in Government departments. Family ties, which are often very old, cut across social boundaries and help in mixing the political, religious and economic spheres, thus reinforcing the cohesion of society. Whatever their status, all Bhutanese are extremely respectful of the monarchy and hope to preserve the country's peace and stability.

People of Bhutan

Although small towns are now beginning to appear, Bhutan is still essentially a rural country. Farmers and stock-breeders represent almost 80% of the total population. In addition to rice, maize and potatoes, the varied climate of Bhutan produces a wide range of cereals and vegetables. High-quality fruit, including many type of citrus, is canned or dried by local industries and sold on the Bhutanese market or exported.

Following double-page: making arak in the courtyard of a house.

Above: Scattered throughout the country, in villages or along the roadside, small local eating-places serve rice and vegetables, arak and tea almost any time of the day... as here in a restaurant at Wamrong on the Samdrup-Jongkhar road. Water is always kept on the boil to make tea, Bhutan's favourite drink. The Bhutanese make two sorts of tea: *ngaja,* which is sweetened and boiled with milk, similar to Indian tea, and *suja,* Tibetan-style buttered, salted tea. It is usually served with *zao,* grilled rice, which is eaten dry or dipped into the tea.

Top right: a typical Bhutanese meal consists of a heap of rice and two or three dishes of vegetables or meat. Like chillies, the national dish, potatoes or mushrooms will be

accompanied by a cheese sauce. Pork fat or dried yak meat complete the feast.

Bottom right: at the end of a meal and indeed at all times of the day, the Bhutanese love to eat a *doma,* a mixture of arec nut and lime folded in a betel leaf. These are often prepared with great - almost ceremonial - care. Offering one is also a mark of friendship or friendliness.

Most Bhutanese still live in semi-autarky, making their own clothes or household articles. Their craftsmanship is of high quality and meets their daily needs. Weaving is done in the home by the women, when they have some spare time between working in the field or around the house. The materials used are cotton, wool, silk (both wild and refined), yak hair and nettle fibre. The dyes, which are prepared by the weavers themselves, are usually plant- or mineral-based.

Above: making a clay pot in a house near Thimphu.

Right: blacksmith in the village of Paro.

Opposite: inside a kitchen near Tongsa and weaving in the Radhi region.

Bhutan is the only country in the world where Mahayana Buddhism (known as *Vajrayana* in its Tantric form) is the official state religion. Certain valleys in Bhutan were first converted to Tantric Buddhism in the middle of the 8th century, while a second phase of conversion spread progressively throughout the country from the 12th century onwards.

The religious schools that exist today in Bhutan are those of the official *drukpa kagyu* "oral transmission" tradition and those of the *nyingmapa* tradition, that of the "ancients", which is derived directly from the teachings of Guru Rinpoche in the 8th century.

The religion practised by people in Bhutan is marked by great veneration for all the divinities of the Buddhist pantheon but also for certain purely local divinities. The Bhutanese regularly visit the country's many temples to make offerings of butter lamps and recite prayers. Rituals are also performed in houses to mark a birth, marriage or death, or to bless the people or the harvest. In a country so deeply influenced by religious belief, a boy from each family would traditionally enter a monastery.

Above: young monks studying in a temple at Punakha *dzong*.

Opposite: a *Brokpa* nomadic breeder from the village of Sakteng visiting a temple in eastern Bhutan.

Following double-page: private ceremony in a house at Zugne, in the Chume valley.

Most of Bhutan's monasteries belong to the *drukpa-kagyu* order, the official state religion. A few in the centre and east of the country also belong to the *nyingmapa* school. In addition to learning the religious texts, young monks receive a basic classical education at the monastery. After a few years' study and depending on their capabilities, the monks are directed towards a purely scholastic activity or to a more artistic one (dancers, musicians, painters, etc.). Some of them will embark on long Buddhist studies in the great religious universities like Tango or Chheri.

Above: reading and learning sacred texts in Simtokha *dzong*.

Right: ceremony in a monastery near Punakha.

Opposite: a monk copies ancient Buddhist texts in gold.

Most of the religious festivals are held once a year in all the great monasteries throughout the country. In a swirl of colour, gods and demons of Buddhist mythology come to life again. These colourful ceremonies, both religious theatre and exorcism ritual, are the most striking testimonies to the deep-rooted faith of Bhutan's society. They are a way of giving lively instruction in the religious philosophy of Buddhism and making the many sacred texts accessible to the uninitiated. Relating the activity of the great saints, they recall the importance of virtuous behaviour and thus play an extremely important didactic role.

From the magical point of view, religious dances are intended to purify the ground, destroy outside enemies, demons and evil spirits, and repel famines, epidemics and wars. But they also help to drive out inner enemies, the ego, obstacles and mental darkness that are so deeply rooted in each being and prevent us from achieving Enlightenment.

Religious festivals

Above: the sound of long trumpets, *dungchen,* and oboes, *gyaling,* announces the entrance of the dancers during the Paro festival.

Right and opposite: the dancers, who are nearly always masked, turn and leap under the fascinated gaze of the crowds of onlookers.
Among these dances, *Dramitse ngacham* celebrates the victory of religion; *Tongsa* festival.

Following pages: *Shanag,* the black hat dance, celebrates the destruction of all enemies of the Doctrine. During this dance, evil spirits are subdued, defeated, imprisoned within a circle and eliminated; Tashigang festival.

Previous pages: the religious festivals usually end with the presentation of the *thongdroel*, an immense patchwork as much as 15 or 20 metres wide, representing the image of Buddha, Guru Rimpoche or Shabdrung. The sight of this *thongdroel* is considered to be a special blessing and it always draws a huge crowd.

Above: apart from the *tsechus*, festivals of masked dances dedicated to Guru Rinpoche, other festivals give thanks to Bhutan's protector Mahakala. One of these, the Punakha festival, celebrates a military victory by Bhutan over the Tibetans more than 300 years ago. Dressed in red and black, the *pazaps* represent the soldiers of Ngawang Namgyel's army. On the last day of the festival, they take part in a great procession

known as *serda*. Flags, banners and streamers form a long, multicoloured ribbon that flaps in the late winter breeze.

Top right: as they leave Punakha dzong, a few *pazaps* make an offering to one of the sacred images of these *tashi gomangs*. In past times, these small portable altars, carried on the back, enabled the Buddha's teachings to be taken into the remotest parts of the mountains, to places where often there was no temple.

Bottom right: the return towards the *dzong* is rowdy and joyous. Shouts of victory are heard all around. This historic day ends with great libations, in which *chang* flows freely.

Religious festivals are held not only in the great *dzongs* of Bhutan but are also often celebrated in the country's remote villages. They sometimes feature rituals and dances unique to the people who live there.

Above left: dance of the *dakini* during the *Mang Kurum* festival at Sakteng. This dance, which is performed early in the morning, invites the celestial divinities to take part in the ceremonies and offer their protection and blessing.

Above right: the *atsara,* rather like the jesters of the Middle Ages, are an essential part of any religious festival in Bhutan. They imitate the monks, make salacious jokes and entertain the public with their clowning. The phallic symbols they wear on the heads or carry in their hands are supposed to distract and thereby ward off evil spirits… as here during the Ura Yakchoe festival.

Opposite: a *dromchoe* celebrated in *Gasa dzong* recalls the arrival of *Shabdrung* Ngawang

Namgyel in Bhutan. Here, in front of a crowd of villagers from Laya, the dancers perform the *Durdag,* the dance of the Lords of the Cremation Grounds.

Following pages: certain religious festivals do not include dances but simply the recital of prayers or carrying of sacred books through the various hamlets in the village. Ritual procession with religious texts, known as *choekhor,* in the village of Merak.

In the west and north, soaring ranges of snow-covered mountains form a natural boundary between Bhutan and the high plateaux of Tibet. They can only be crossed by a few passes at more than 5000 metres, which were formerly used as trading routes between the regions to the north and south of the Himalayas. Most of the summits have never been climbed and the existing maps are fairly approximate. In spite of the harsh climate, though, these high valleys offer the ever-changing spectacle of grandiose mountain ranges covered in everlasting snow and ice. Changing colour at different times of the day, sometimes even appearing to change shape, the great peaks are an awesome, captivating sight.

Right: Jomolhari (7320 m), with the ancient ruined fortress of Jangothang at its feet.

Following double-pages: Jitchu Drake (6794 m), its magnificent ridges running northwards from the Jomolhari massif.

Mountains and trek

Above: the village of Laya is situated on a small plateau at almost 4000 metres, at the edge of the forest and high pasture. The stone houses are grouped into little hamlets, with people and animals living under the same roof. A steep wooden staircase, or sometimes just a simple ladder, leads from the ground floor cattle shed to the first floor living quarters.

Right: the inhabitants of Laya came from Tibet many centuries ago, but they have kept their own customs and costumes. The young girls and women wear an amusing conical hat made of bamboo. At a very early age, they proudly start to sport this distinctive head-dress, which, along with their many pieces of jewellery, often mixed with spoons and silver coins, clearly shows that they belong to the clan.

Opposite: Gasa *dzong* in the early morning, dominated by the dazzling snows of Gangbum (6500 m).

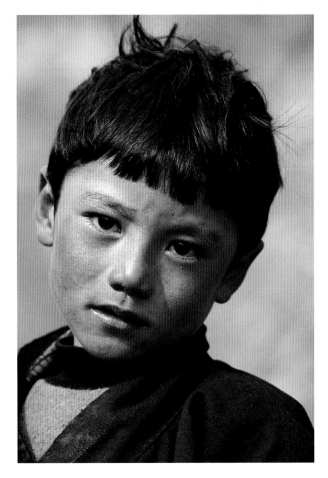

Above: the remotest and most inaccessible
regions of Bhutan are those of Lunana. It
takes many days' walking, with several
passes at more than 5000 metres to be
crossed, before one reaches Chözo *dzong*
and Thangza. Huge glaciers descend from
summits rising to more than 7000 m,
ending in numerous glacial lakes of
infinitely varied colours.

Right: the elegant peaks of Masang Kang
(7200 m), the holy mountain of the Layap.

Opposite: one of the many lakes in Lunana,
whose delicate colours range from
emerald to turquoise.

Following pages: just below Gophu La pass
(5350 m), one comes upon the magnificent
lake Tsorim.

Previous pages: a caravan of yaks crossing Gothang La (4255 m).

Despite a harsh climate and endless winters, these isolated spots of Lunana were the favourite destination of people coming from Tibet. Men and women learnt to live there, forging their character on the anvil of this stark, uncompromising environment… The barbarous appearance and wild expressions of the inhabitants give some indication of the difficulty of living in this spot at the end of the earth. Their lifestyle and customs are those of mountain folk. They raise yaks, turning to farming for just a short period in the summer when the barley and black wheat have enough heat to grow. That is also the time when some of them depart with their herds in search of better pasture, living in black tents made of yak hair. In the winter, they devote themselves to handicrafts or go and live in the villages lower down the mountainside where the climate is not so severe. They can then do a little trading with the villagers from the surrounding areas.

Above: nestling at the foot of the Phurbu Kang, the village of Chözo *dzong* is isolated for months during the winter.

Opposite: any trek in Bhutan takes the traveller through magnificent forests filled with a wide variety of species. The autumn offers an infinite palette of colours and smells, where scented pines blend with the yellowing larches and blue Himalayan firs. Huge mosses hang from the bending trunks and mingle with the broad leaves of ferns. A vision of beauty that is a source of peace, well-being and inspiration.

For more information about Robert Dompnier's photographic work on Bhutan, consult:

www.photos-bhutan.com

Recommended reading list

- **ADAMS Barbara,** Traditional Textiles of Bhutan, White Orchid, Bangkok, 1984.

- **ACHARYA Sanjay**, Bhutan: Kingdom in the Himalayas, Lustre Press/Roli books, New-Delhi, 1999.

- **ARIS Michael,** The Raven Crown, Serindia, London, 1994.

- **ARMINGTON Stan,** Bhutan, Lonely Planet, London-Melbourne-Paris, 1998, 2002.

- **BARKER David,** Designs of Bhutan, White Lotus, Bangkok, 1985

- **BARTHOLOMEW Mark,** Thunder Dragon: Textiles from Bhutan, Shikôsha Publishing Co., Tokyo, 1985.

- **BEAN Suzanna. & MYERS Diana,** From the land of the Thunder Dragon: textiles arts of Bhutan, Serindia-Peabody Essex Museum, London, 1994.

- **CHANG DORJI,** The clear mirror of Archery in Bhutan, Chang Dorji, Khasadrapchu, 2001.

- **CROSSETTE Barbara,** So close to heaven, the vanishing Buddhist kingdoms of the Himalayas, Vintage Departures, Random House, 1995.

- **DOMPNIER Robert,** Bhutan, Kingdom of the Dragon, Local Colour, Hong Kong, 1999.

- **DORJI WANGMO WANGCHUCK (H.M. Ashi),** Of rainbows and Clouds, the life of Yab Ugyen Dorji as told to his daughter, Serindia, London, 1998.

- **DOWMAN Keith,** The Divine madman. The sublime Life & Songs of Drukpa Kunley, Rider Co, London, 1980.

- **GREGSON Jonathan,** Kingdoms beyond the clouds : journeys in search of the Himalayan Kings, Macmillan, London, 2000.

- **HARDING Sarah,** The Life and revelations of Pema Lingpa, Snow Lion, Ithaca-Boulder, 2003..

- **JAGAR DORJI,** Lhop, A tribal Community in South Western Bhutan, and its survival through time, NIE, Paro, 2003.

- **KARMA URA,** The Hero with a thousand eyes, Karma Ura, Thimphu, 1995.

- **KARMA URA,** The ballad of Pemi Tshewang Tashi, Karma Ura, Thimphu, 1996.

- **KARMA URA,** Deities, archers and planners in the era of decentralization, Karma Ura, Thimphu, 2004.

- **KUNZANG CHODEN,** Folktales of Bhutan, White Lotus, Bangkok, 1993.

- **KUNZANG CHODEN,** Bhutanese tales of the yeti, White Lotus, Bangkok, 1997.

- **KUNZANG CHODEN,** The circle of Karma, Penguin/Zuban, New-Delhi, 2005.

- **KUNZANG THINLEY & DOMPNIER Robert,** The Folk Heritage Museum, Jomo Publications, Thimphu, 2005.

- **NISHIOKA Keiji & NAKAO,** Sasuke Flowers of Bhutan, Asahi Shimbum, Tokyo, 1984.

- **POMMARET Françoise,** Bhutan, (Guidebook) Odyssey, Hong-Kong (1991), 2005.

- **RINZIN RINZIN,** The talisman of good fortune and other stories from rural Bhutan, Rinzin Rinzin, Thimphu 2002.

- **SCHICKLGRUBER Christian & POMMARET Françoise,** Bhutan : Mountain Fortress of the Gods, Serindia, London, 1997.

- **SITHEL DORJI (Dasho),** The origin and description of Bhutanese mask dances, KMT Press, Thimphu, 2001.

- **SOLVERSON Howard,** The Jesuit & the Dragon, Robert Davies Publ. Outremont, 1995.

- **SONAM KINGA,** Gaylong Sumdar Tashi: Songs of Sorrow, CAPSS, Education Division, Thimphu, 1998. 2nd Ed. CBS, Thimphu, 2002.

- **SONAM KINGA,** Speaking statues, flying rocks. Writings on Bhutanese history, myths and culture, DSB, Thimphu, 2005.